Lydia Believes

Acts 16:13–15 for children

Written by Stephenie Hovland

Illustrated by Michelle Dorenkamp Repa

CONCORDIA PUBLISHING HOUSE • SAINT LOUIS

Lydia walked to the river to pray.
Worshiping God was her plan for the day.
Some knew her faith in the God of the Jews,
But most sought her fabric with violet hues.

Lydia's beautiful cloth was unique,
Purple and treasured by all who would seek
Fabric for royalty near Philippi.
It was admired by all who walked by.

She was in business to sell goods most days.
But on the Sabbath Day, she came to praise
Yahweh, the Father, who promised to send
A Savior, upon whom all people depend.

Visitors joined them and soon shared Good News,
Telling of Jesus, the King of the Jews.
Paul spoke the Word of God clearly to them.
The Spirit of God was with women and men.

God worked His Gospel in Lydia's heart.
After it rooted, she wanted to start
To follow the call of the Lord Jesus Christ,
Who for the world's sin had paid the
full price.

Lydia believed in the truth of God's Word
And came to faith through what she had heard.
Baptized along with her servants and kin,
Her new life in Jesus then did begin.

"If you have judged me
  as faithful and true,
Come to my dwelling,
  where I can serve you."
Lydia eagerly gave
  of God's grace,
Welcoming Christians
  to stay at her place.

Paul and his friends were invited to stay
Whenever they needed to meet or to pray.
Accepting the offer to visit and share,
They made plans for ministry while they
were there.

Europe's first churches began at that time,
But many thought worshiping Jesus a crime.
Challenges came to those households of faith.
Lydia offered a place that was safe.

Lydia opened her home and her heart.
We, too, can follow a woman so smart.
She worked her business of selling dyed cloth,
While caring for those from nearby
    and far off.

Lydia's life—an example to see:
Strong faith combined with humility.
God gave her talents to use as a way
To bless other people day after day.

Serving the Lord was where she truly shone,
Worshiping Christ and making Him known.
She opened her house as a place to pray
To the true God, who sent Jesus to save.

Years before, Jesus had made a command,
"Go make disciples in every land,
Baptizing them in the Father, the Son,
The Spirit—the great, holy God, Three in One."

Lydia showed us we need not go far.
We can have missions wherever we are!
God's Great Commission is meant for us all,
Sharing His Word as we answer His call.

Dear Parent,

Although Lydia's story in the Book of Acts is brief, Luke includes it as an example of how Jesus' promise of salvation and the work of the Holy Spirit are for all people.

During his second missionary journey, around AD 50, Paul traveled to the European continent to preach the Gospel to Gentiles. In Philippi, in what is now Greece, Paul joined a small group of Jews who were gathered to worship God. He preached to them about Jesus, the promised Savior. Lydia, a Gentile believer, was there. She came to faith and was baptized. She convinced Paul and those with him (Silas and Timothy) to be guests in her home, which then became the headquarters of Paul's ministry in that area.

Lydia is thought to be the first European on record to be converted to the Christian faith. This is significant in itself. But her greater legacy is that she was a woman of influence. Her position as a merchant put Lydia in contact with many people. That meant she could—and likely did—share her faith with them.

Like Lydia, we can share our faith and serve the Lord wherever we are—at home, at work, at school—and trust that God's will is gracious and will be done.

The Editor